JELLIED EELS & MULTI-CULTURALISM

A POEM COLLECTION ON MODERN LIFE IN THE UK

By Chris Statham

Also By

THE UGLY GLORY SERIES

THE MAN IN THE MIRROR - A collection on male mental health
FRIDAY NIGHT FEVER – A collection on booze, nightlife & the battle with sobriety
JELLIED EELS & MULTI-CULTURALISM – A collection on modern life in the UK
THIS IS WHY WE MET - A collection on dating, friends with benefits & sex workers
MY NORTH STAR - A collection on love, divorce & finding a way forward
JUST ANOTHER MARTIAN CAT LIVING IN BASILDON - A collection on exploring creativity & the world
LIFE PRIRATE – A collection on life, death & all that jazz

AFRONIA SERIES

Crying for Afronia (Volume 1)
Escape from Afronia (Volume 2)
Dying for Afronia (Volume 3)
Afronia Rising (Volume 4)
Developing Afronia (Volume 5)

PROSE, POEM AND PICTURES SERIES

7 Days in 1 Week (Volume 1)
12 Months in a Year (Volume 2)
10 Years in a Decade (Volume 3)

OTHER FICTION NOVELS

18 Reflections and 3 Statements of Relief
Paperback Writer

DEDICATION

To Brooklyn, Barney, Bella and Brenden

Copyright and Disclaimer

Author – Chris Statham
Sketches by Hezdean Chinthengah
Published by **www.creativityxroads.com**
Jellied eels, 978-0-9955196-4-0

CONTENTS

FORWARD

My formative years were the post Nirvana mid-90s. A time when football became the game for all the family, pubs and clubs could stay open all hours, and low-cost airlines made their irreversible entrance. The conversation moving beyond whether you were a Prince or Michael Jackson fan to the iconic Blur or Oasis debate. My late teens, the Cool Britannia years, revolved around clubbing in Ibiza and larging it every weekend. Underworld's "Born Slippy" was our anthem and Loaded magazine our bible.

I'm part of the "Lager, lager, lager" generation. I'm not a hipster who wears skinny jeans, ironic glasses, bow ties, drinks fancy coffees, Snapchats and Instagrams. I thought when I left school, if I worked hard enough for long enough, I could have a career and my house would be my castle. However, just as I was getting some money together, the 2008 financial crash shattered my dreams.

I'm a Brit in my mid-40s, Empire, The Royal Family and Commonwealth conjure up images of former grandeur. Winston Churchill, Nelson and Elizabeths I & II are not only historical idols but also integral parts of our cultural identity. We are a rebellious, cussed island that doesn't like being told what to do… that's why we voted Brexit and gave Hitler a bloody nose. We are a land of entrepreneurs, inventors and creativity. Some of our most successful exports include, The Beatles and Vivienne Westwood via Damien Hirst, John Betjeman, and the Bard from Shropshire.

The socio-economic divide in the UK can largely be attributed to a democratic deficit. The link between MPs and constituents is broken. Those who inhabit Westminster are part of an out-of-touch bubble that kowtows to corporate overlords and black money. They no longer represent the majority and who are only just about managing, JAMS as Theresa May coined. Today's politicians have virtually nothing in-common, whether education, holidays or work experience with their voters. Faces who see Big Ben on a regular basis are not familiar with the hardships of teachers, military personnel, doctors and nurses, or those who know what it's like to drive a tractor or fish for a living. Instead, many are career politicians who have boarded he great gravy train. Even journalists, who are meant to keep the elite accountable, now settle for soundbites rather than being inquisitive about the country they live in.

This collection of poems delves into modern Britain. It examines how we glorify the past, are living through a combustible present of a weakening economy, climate change and socio-economic gap-widening and have a very uncertain future. The poems examine questions faced by many Brits. How do we forge a national identity? Is a work life balance possible? Is there genuine or fake acceptance of difference, whether religious, ethnic or sexual? And finally, how does technology shape our present and what part will it play in the future?

WHERE I COME FROM

For the past 25 years, ever since Prince Blair had his 1997 coronation, we've lived in a political landscape where the two main parties, Labour and Conservative, have been saying pretty much the same thing to secure the grey vote. It's consensus politics that revolves around back rubbing between the powerful, the influential and the financially independent. No wonder much of the country is apathetic to those in Westminster. On almost every issue the country is more divided than when I was a nipper. There are increasing clashes between the blue rinse brigade and millennials. The haves hiding their wealth offshore while the have nots struggle. Employees are grateful they're not giggers. The polarisation between Remoaners and Brexiters, COVID-19 vaccinated and anti-vaxers. Populists versus liberals, elites, progressive, immigrants and many other socio-economic groups. Why is this? In my opinion, most politicians are a bunch of lying, self-serving bastards who care nothing about those they are supposed to represent. There main concern is keeping their positions of power to exploit the system for personal gain. Who can forget the scandalous expenses claimed by a Tory grandee in summer 2013 and which included a grand-and-a-half for a floating duck house! You can't make this shit up; it's beyond belief. Then there was the deceit surrounding the Gulf War dirty dossier, and inumerous scandals involving lobbying and cash-for-questions. These poems look st the UK today.

Made in the UK

A land of the proudest traditions,
an island not conquered since William,
the home of kings and queens and where the sun
never set over the Empire.

Henry and his six wives.
Shakespeare and Chaucer.
18th and 19th century greats of invention, innovation and the written word.
Churchill,
bulldogs,
1966 and all that.
Charles, Di... and Camilla.
The global phenomena that is the
Premier League.

A mongrel nation of Brummies,
Cockneys,
Geordies,

The UK is a digital present with
analogue past.
Brits glorify a black and white yesterday and are in awe of the one true
god, capitalism.

Mancs and Scousers,
the union no longer living the European dream
but following the American one where anybody
can achieve anything under the umbrella of a
crumbling welfare state safety net.

The UK is a country where you can love who you
want,
worship at any altar,
be who you want to be,
do what you want to do,
fill your potential or try and fail,
but also inequality.

My Generation

I'm neither the generation of tradition nor technology;
I'm Generation X.

I straddle the analogue and digital divide whereby technology equals efficiency not a way of life.

I remember my first mobile,
my first taste of the web and black and white TV.
It was an internet-free childhood.
Tinder was for fires not a swipe-based hook-up app.

We climbed trees, played soldiers
and chased for a kiss.
I was brought up, when porn meant bat-eared magazines in sheds not downloadable clips.
My after-school viewing:
The A-Team and He-Man,
Grange Hill and Danger Mouse;
I played Sonic the Hedgehog on a Mega Drive.

The Falklands and Gulf Wars,
Home and Away,
Kylie and Jason dominated my screen together
with Gazza and his World Cup tears,
FA Cup broken leg and,
redemption from lurid headlines when flicking over a Scottish head.

Baddiel, Skinner and Stato singing Three Lions my abiding memory of the summer of 96,
my transition into the adult world.

I just missed out on acid house,
grunge, disco and punk,
but got The Space Cowboy,
Blur and Oasis,

Cool Britannia.
The superstar DJ and the mega nightclub.
Larging it every weekend with the lads,

"Lager, lager, lager" our anthem,
TFI Fridays the starting pistol to euphoria.

Pierce Bronson was our James Bond,
Trainspotting our film.
Loaded our magazine,
Princess DI in Paris,
the Twin Towers falling,
our: Where Were You? moments.
Lehman Brothers bankruptcy and the 2008 financial crash…
the economic millstone around our austerity necks.

I don't have the uncertainty of Millennials in the gig economy with zero-hour contracts.
I'm not a metro-sexual who drinks craft beer nor a hipster who goes to cereal bars.
I don't have the certainty of Boomers-
jobs for life,
free education and health,
pensions.
I'm a British male of Generation X caught between tradition and modernity,
a house is but a liberal economic fairy-tale and not my castle.

I was brought up in an analogue past,
I'm living a digital present and have an unknown future.

My Politics...

Politics has nothing to do with me!

I have no representation from vanilla politicians,
my voice not heard.
The only words I know:
austerity,
gig economy,
financial insecurity.

75K only, MPs whinge.
Allowances and cash for questions.
Fiddling the books for a living salary.
Consultancy and directorships on the side as they
guzzle champagne with city cronies.

They have,
I have not.
Their want,
is just a want not like my necessity;
inequality,
this our social divide.

Apathetic is my world...
salaries never stirred,
house prices escalate,
credit cards accumulate.

My democratic right wasted,
no party represents my aspirations and fears,
daily challenges.

So I say, fuck'em all:
political snobs,

pollsters and commentators,
but most of all,
bleedin' politicians.

If I voted,
my vote would go to Mr or Mrs Anti-establish-
ment,
someone who knows the price of a pint,
milk or beer,
who has controversial ideas,
are tree shakers that will drain the swamp and dis-
rupt the status quo.

Politics,
it's a white-collar hustle.

Climate Change

There is Brexit,
Ukraine,
but this is moving deckchairs on the Titanic,
a wilful blind-eye,
defying logic to make money,
make the political roundabout spin while the world
is burning,
hurricanes destroying,
cyclones circling,
tornados destructing,
droughts, famine causing.

Climate change is coming,
times, they are already a changing,
this not a Dylan reference…
the world tomorrow not what we know today!

I've lived a life,
seen the world,
loved a woman,
made my successes,
commiserated my failures,
but my kids have not lived yet,
our decisions reducing theirs.

Lobbyists,
political prissy cats,
dark money determining futures;

they are unethical,
immoral-
just plain wrong.

It's time to build Noah's ark,
heed the warnings,
believe the science,
trust positive solutions,
make radical change,
have hope.

We live in one world,
we are one people,
we must find an equitable future or we're all done
for,
the Jenga tower of modern-life tilting,
crumbling,
falling,
smashing on our avarice as the environment,
our hope,
we wilfully killing.

We must fight for a future that is equitable,
supply chains bio-degradable,
ecosystems sustainable,
humanity habitable,
all living in harmony.

We are One

I was born in the UK but lived Berlin this week-
end.
We are the same continent
but vastly different identities,
cultures,
outlook on life and levels of acceptance.

Berlin,
the city no one can ever fully know,
the city I feel I know so well,
a new home to my soul,
where anyone can be anything,
where all goes.

When I walk a British high street I see betting
shops,
Poundland,
bakeries,
takeaways and closed signs;
in Berlin,
the atmosphere,
culture,
openness so different.

The U-Bahn and S-Bahn are frequent and on time,
affordable and clean,
not overcrowded,
this, the underground hell I normally know.

People work pierced or tattooed,
suits or conformity,
each free to do what feels natural as long as the
job gets done.

Alcohol is everywhere,
every shop selling a cold one.
Drinking on the streets,
not a problem;
there is no violence,
puking or overwhelming police presence;
Berliners understand respect for all.

Berlin,
a city of cafes and independent bars,
specialist shops,
endless parks and street festivals,
entrepreneurs going about their business,
living their passions,
out of sight and mind of corporate behemoths.

In Berlin,
there is freedom in the truest sense.
No discrimination of colour,
sexuality or creed.
Where all are one family,
all God's children,
rich or poor,
black or white,
all making their way,
finding a path through life,
learning who they are,
what they like,
what makes them tick,
what makes us thee.

Quiet or loud,
god or godless,
straight or gay,
all are accepted,
each to their own as long as acceptance of pecca-
dilloes,

preferences,
individuality,
beliefs and idiosyncrasies.

In Berlin,
follow the simple rule,
respect others no matter race or religion,
income level, age or sexual orientation.

Berlin,
the city of personal change,
the city of love;

where there is the power of humanity,
living,
what brings people together greater than drives
part,
where, prejudices get shattered daily,

Berlin,
remain blessed,
I, a proud European not little Englander want to
say,
Ich bin ein Berli

Raise the Flag and Man the Barricades

Raise the flag and man the barricades.

Brothers and sisters,
you,
who should be by our sides,
why are you fighting reality,
forgetting inequality,
defending others prosperity?

We,
the masses,
must decide our future,
the fate of our land,
the way we will govern and be governed;
this is democracy.

So, I say,
man the barricades against hypocrites and cowards,
those not willing to fight the good fight,
who want security but risk freedom.

Man the barricades,
don't be sheep kowtowing to the elite,
wolves,
their crock of gold that is a crock of shit,
lies and deceit to trap you in economic servitude.

Man the barricades.

Our time is now for our future,
our freedom,
to snap out of subservience.

Man the barricades.

You can only live if you are willing to die!
Now is the time to decide your fate,
the fate of your family.
the fate of the nation.

Join with me brothers and sisters,
my children and fellow parents and fight for your rights,
fight for the light,
raise the flag and man those barricades!

MULTI-CULTURALISM

Discourse for the past decade has been dominated about Eastern European immigration, Brexit and asylum seekers from further afield. This has been the background to fuel the cultural wars, pitting multi-culturalism against a more insular "Little England" mentality, this rather than the traditional divide of old vs the young, and haves vs the underprivileged. Another significant development has been the growth of Atheism, this raising question whether spirituality and religion are soon to be a thing of the past. While I don't have faith, I see friends and relations get an inner strength from their God(s). and then there's racism. Back in my teenage years, TV and magazines usually showed black men and women in a derogatory light: the thug, the happy go lucky, the chancer, the drug dealer, the big-dick ladies' man, the crackwhore; stereotypes that eroded trust. There were a few acceptable or tolerated types: the black man with a cheeky grin and infectious laugh. The highly-educated black woman. Thankfully, times have moved on, the UK now truly multi-cultural, with appropriate freedoms so that everyone can express their identities, while acknowledging institutional racism in areas such as the police, higher education and sports, to name but a few still continue.

Despite the shifting demographics over the past half century, there has been no post-race utopia since Prince Harry and Megan Markle baptised their first child. There is a moratorium on discussing race and religion; if you bring up racism in conversation, you're considered a racist. Minorities are often accused of playing the race or religion card. My point of view, saying someone is black, brown, white, yellow etc. is stating a factual characteristic. It only becomes racist and abhorrent when negative connotations, stereotypes, prejudices are added. As for religion, everyone should be free to worship who they please. It's the job of government to ensure there are freedoms and equality for all.

Immigration

I run from poverty and war,
corruption and nepotism.

I have left my friends,
my wife,
but most heartbreakingly of all,
my children behind.

My heart is broken but I will endure.
I'll walk across deserts dodging bandits.
I'll dare the God of the seas to take me.
I'll walk over snowy mountains passes.
I'll do anything in search for a better life
for those dearest to me.

My new country,
my new life,
the people with their rights and their wrongs,
everything foreign to me.

As I walk your beautiful streets,
I notice everything not available at home:
freedoms,
rights,
hope!

I'm not respected as a human wanting to do what's best for my family;
this is my choice,
my destiny,
and I will endure in my search for peace and opportunity,
prosperity.

Hope,
all that keeps me going.
Hope,
for a brighter tomorrow.
Hope,
the dreams for my family will come true.

Waves of The Same Sea

I'm like you.
I have the same hopes and desires,
as you,
the same fears,
as you,
but different challenges….

We are fundamentally waves of the same sea,
leaves of the same tree,
flowers of the same garden,
but I have a different god,
a different colour of skin,
a different motherland that I call home…
that I've left behind.

I made sacrifices you can't imagine,
loved ones abandoned and dreams crushed to come here.
But I'm greeted with no geniality,
this my reality;
my decision most times seems utmost futility as I'm treated like criminality,
a hated immigrant,
a despised Jonny foreigner.

Asylum seeker, spat at me,
by you,
you,
who have no idea who I am,
where I'm from or the life I've left behind.

You,
with your insecurities
prejudices,
outright hostilities,
who gives to charities,
to ease your bestialities,
to remove your accountabilities.

Keep your shamefaced liabilities
as while we are both humans,
our lives are different galaxies with no meaningful
similarities even though we are fundamentally
waves of the same sea.

Mixed Race Britain

White and black make grey.
Yellow and blue is green.

Brown and white,
caramel,
mocha,
love.

Our children,
born of parents from different worlds,
cultures and ethnicities,
get the best of both.

Darwin would be happy:
the creation of such strength from difference.

Religion

Religion–
the spark of war,
a convenient excuse for chaos,
domination and extermination.

Religion–
the Mother of all evils,
exploitation of the masses;
crowd control by other means.

Religion–
the greatest trick the elite ever pulled...
Worship one God and I'll set the rules which favour me!

Religion –
an evil corrupting the soul,
taking hope and sodomising Faith.

Black or White Jesus?

A holy man from the land of sand…
or the North Pole?

Blue eyes and skin whiter than snow,
the sun He created…
not darkening his body?

OR…
Jesus,
a good man,
high of morals,
ethics to be proud.

A man of Jerusalem,
beard and sandals,
of dessert dates and donkeys…

Why should white be the colour of
purity, freedom, honesty and peace,
and black,
evil and all that's bad.

European, African or Arab,
you tell me?
All I know,
in a white world it's not possible to have a black
Jesus.

Ramadan Kareem

Ramadan Kareem
Brother and sisters fast from food,
water,
sex and smoking.

Practice self-discipline,
spiritual reflection,
empathy for the less fortunate and
consider how to improve.

It's a time for feasting,
rejoicing in the iftar,
being generous with charity and uniting with
family.

To discover the simple joys of life,
being spiritually reborn,
reclaiming your soul and following the teaching of
Islam.
Eid Mubarak

Forced Marriage

I'm 16 years old,

I've been married 5 months and,
I'm 7 months' pregnant.

I can't rejoice in my heart for the life growing
within.
No one should be happy for this abomination of a
marriage that is dressed up as love –
my husband,
quadruple my age,
triple my slender weight.

I was abducted while working in the fields,
taken to a cave in the hills,
raped and disgraced.

This wasn't my first time though…
I was initiated five years ago.
Culture dictated I marry the father of my unborn
child,
for family honour!?!

What is that?
For my family?
For me?
For my rapist husband?

I hoped for romance and wooing,
not forced sexual intercourse.
I hoped my child would be born from love,
into a loving family –
not physical and mental terror,
pain and hurt.

Naïve me in the ways of men.
Naïve me in the ways of cultural traditions of my
motherland,
where my story is just gossip and not a crime,
where I'm not a victim,
where I have to accept as I have no family support
or recourse via government institutions.

But I refuse to accept and acknowledge the prison
I'm in as my mind is free,
my adopted land giving me freedoms,
rights.

I will escape my walls through my words.
I will reveal my injustices so I can live in peace.
Through my mental fortitude,
I will love my child as no love was shown to me.

I will create societal change by telling my story,
by sharing my suffering,
by holding the wrongs in my life,
accountable.

By being honest,
baring my soul,
hopefully,
other teenage girls won't suffer as I did,
still do.

Everyone has a meaning to life and this is mine.
I will rise like a phoenix and soar in my new coun-
try.

Division

I am me and you are you;
skin and religion should not divide!
But consider this:
if you're not white you're considered black.

White girls like Latino guys,
Asian guys like black chicks;
is this stereotyping or truth?
Jungle fever or simple attraction?
Racism or reality?

I'm black
you're brown,
she's yellow,
he's white,
but we're an indistinct rainbow in the eyes of the
capitalist Man,
nothing but consumers to unicorn gods.

I'm Sikh,
you Christian,
he Jew
she Muslim,
but we should be one,
united,
all our blood runs red,
hearts beats sparks.

We are equal under the sun and stars.
There is no shadow of the Man in the clouds but
there is one who shapes our lives,
the Man who only cares about the green.

What unites must be more than divides.

We all live for tomorrow,
but should remember our common past.
It is those who don't understand,
don't want unity,
who try to sow division through our present,
who don't want us to retire,
but slave,
makes us social media jealous,
It is they who contrive not for contrition,
but attrition,
hate.

We should not let anger enter our souls or destroy
our humanity.
It is us,
we,
who can determine our present,
our future,
our joint fate no matter our colour,
our religion.

Clarity in Chaos

The spic,
the wop,
the black, Arab and Jew,
what do they know of us?
What do they know of our culture,
our language,
our way of life?

They come with their families,
take our jobs,
don't integrate,
don't accept our culture.

Boys in gangs terrify grannies on buses.
They live in their ghettos,
go to their mosques,
speak their monkey language and rape our women.

We are not respected in our own country;
we must form a militia,
a vigilante army to keep our land pure.

But,
what the fuck?

My life's turned upside down.

I'm beaten to a pulp...
by whites.
Saved by someone,
I don't even know what to call him?
I've always referred to them as sand niggers.
But he saved my ass,
a good Samaritan to me,
I,
a white devil to him...
or so I thought,
what I have always been told,
led to believe.

I'm confused,
I'm lost,

my life upside down but my soul now free,
my conscience finally clear.

Has my hatred and insecurities made me the loser?
Not accepting others for who they are,
Judging on the colour of skin,
the language they speak,
the God they pray to...
following preconceptions I'd been taught rather
than looking at the soul within,
the person they are.

It's not too late,
never too late to right wrongs,
love not hate my different skinned brothers from
other mothers.

This man,
stranger,
not just my saviour but my light,
salvation,
I, learning a lesson,
I thought could never be taught.

Acceptance

Hindu or Muslim,
Gentile or Jew,
we are all one under the eye of God,
whichever god...
or gods they might be.

We all bleed the same blood.
We all need food and water to live.
We all need the love of friends, family and
strangers.
We should all be accepting not intolerant of
difference.

Faith means different things to different people.
Religious doctrines each have their specifics.
Some will pray at the mosque, the synagogue, the
church,
others simply in their mind's eye,
and some have no faith but believe in the human
consciousness,
their own understanding of right and wrong,
their pathway through life.

But we are one people,
our similarities more than differences;
there's no reason not to love thy neighbour.

Each person has the right to believe in what they
may;
It's not for anyone to criticise life choices with
bigoted opinion.

We are individuals,
brought up in an environment unique to each.
Nature and nurture,
one not better than the other,
just different circumstances;
be grateful for what you have,
not what you don't.

Learn and educate yourself about others-
ignorance is no excuse,
it says more about you than the target of your ire;
be a lover who accepts not intolerant hater.

Populism

Populist rhetoric welcomes friends
and kick out foes.
To make the UK great again…
but fuck the rest of the world.

I say,
don't look inwards,
put humanity first.
Help those most at need,
not bombast isolationism.

Love thy neighbour.
Appreciate the differences that makes us stronger
not weaker,
understand,
that diversity should breed creativity not contempt.

Learn from others and don't scorn variety.
Embrace what you don't know rather than submit to ignorance.

Strength is in the pack,
so embrace the weakest,
don't humiliate or bully the defenceless.

Lead by example by building bridges not walls;
together,
we can make the world great again.

CHASING THE GREEN

A businessman is walking along the beach when he sees a fisherman lying on the sand. Why are you not fishing? he enquires. The fisherman sits up and replies nonchalantly, I will soon. If you work hard, the businessman smugly persists, then you will be rich and can relax. What do you think I'm doing now! The fisherman states with a shrug of his shoulders before lying back down on the sand. I wish I'd heard this parable many years ago. As a Brit growing up in the era of Thatcherism, I was fed the myth, that money-chasing was the only path to success, that success equals happiness and, merely having enough was insufficient. We are told to plan from a young age, believing that a 25-year mortgage and pension is the epitome of sensible.

There is a vast disconnect between the fully employed and those living gig-gig, contract-to-contract. Central bankers and macro-economists have little idea of the weekly home-economics calculations of the majority Most people are hard-working, honest, salt-of-the-earth types striving to make it through the day, the week, till the end of the month and their pay-packet… only to repay accumulated debts, have a few beers and start the miserable, weary debt-cycle process again. Those who buck the system, carve their own life paths, whether entrepreneur, gigger or consultant, face an arduous journey. If you believe this is for you, go with your eyes wide open and embrace challenges fearlessly while you navigate the unknown and downright tricky. Remember, an idea is only as good as the sweat, toil, perseverance, motivation, communication, planning and a hundred other attributes. You can be a superstar inventor, but, if you can't take it to market then you don't have a viable business. Ideas are cheap and accomplishment comes from hard work more than genius. As Newton's third law of motion, states, for every action there is an equal and opposite reaction. This principle holds especially true when starting and running a business.

The upcoming collection of poems delves into the various avenues of earning a livelihood be it through employment, consultancy, crime or entrepreneurship. Additionally, it explores the essence of leadership.

The Fire Within

I burn with ambition.
I burn to give my children all that I have plus more.
I burn to make my parents proud.
I burn to be a role model for those who need heroes,
someone to aspire to.

I burn to set a good example and singe my fingers at times.
I'm not faultless, just human,
aiming high, often falling short.

I want to learn from experience,
to turn failure into success,
to be the shining-light others follow.

I burn in frustration that life's not always easy,
that success doesn't come overnight,
that I don't live up to my ideals.

I collect the tinder of life and add the spark of experience,
so that I can be the bonfire on a hilltop,
a beacon of inspiration to those I love.

Dream Job

I sent my CV,
had two interviews and signed the contract.

The morning of the first day,
I bounded up the office stairs like an excited Labrador,
I, full of gleeful anticipation.

New colleagues and clients to meet,
projects to start,
knowledge and experiences to gain;
my dream job had come true.

The first month passed in a flash;
probation, a formality.
I was Mr High Energy full of ideas,
insights and inspiration;
I was living my dream.

Six months in,
I still had motivation,
but what was once exciting now humdrum.
My role forever changing,
not sure of my future,
I, a ragdoll for management.

Time passes and now I stare at grey walls.
My motivation vanished,
my energy sucked dry,
my output now the bare minimum,
I only continue so as to pay bills.

I follow the minute hand on my watch waiting for the
morning break, lunch,
afternoon break, home,
not caring if I'm fired,
my dream turned nightmare.

I Don't Like Mondays

Tell me why I don't like Mondays,
I want to shoot the whole day down.

I wake tired,
shit, shave, shower,
get dressed,
go to work.
14 hours later back home,
eat, go to sleep,
repeat.

Tell me why I don't like Mondays,
I want to shoot the whole day down.

The definition of insanity:
doing the same thing and expecting a different
outcome;
I must be insane.

Tell me why I don't like Mondays,
I want to shoot the whole day down.

Tiredness, a fact of modern life.
Different diet, more exercise, more sleep;
the doctor's orders tremors,
minor ripples not the earthquakes demanded,
needed.

Tell me why I don't like Mondays,
I want to shoot the whole day down.

Who decides:
work 12-hour days,
commute,
fret about mortgages and credit cards?

Tell me why I don't like Mondays,
I want to shoot the whole day down.

There's no running away from work,
no lottery win allowing me to drink away
my misery,

to not face the facile reality of work,
loneliness,
alcoholism,
dependency;
there is no choice but to work tomorrow.

Tell me why I don't like Mondays,
I want to shoot the whole day down.

I should become my own boss,
free in my mind,
live my dream,
choose when and how I work,
fulfil my passions,
move from the city to the countryside.

Tell me why I don't like Mondays,
I want to shoot the whole day down.

To cure tiredness and lethargy,
I should get a dog,
move to a new country,
start a new job,
these, tsunamis of change.

Tell me why I don't like Mondays,
I want to shoot the whole day down.

Phoenix from the Ashes

"You're fired,"
Fred the fuck, informs me,
this a bolt from the blue;
am I in Trump land?

"What the hell?" I ask.
"Great appraisal last month,"
I remind him.
"You can't turn my life upside down, again"
I plead thinking of family.

"Automation!"
the heartless bastard clarifies.

I'm marched out the office,
head held high but heart sunken,
uncomprehending,
embarrassed,
dehumanized for a robot.

Motherfuckers, with their business bullshit,
jargon, Fred thinks,
makes him sound clever.
Saying, "Its a no brainer,
let's touch base.
It's already on my radar to discuss the low-hanging fruit."

Going on about,
"Thinking outside the box,
blue sky thinking and blank sheets of paper to address the elephant in the room,
to win hearts and minds."

Well, screw Fred and this blasted company;
this is the wake-up call I needed-
I'll rise like a phoenix.

Living a Fast Food Life

My life is dashing here to there,
one meeting to another,
no time to stop,
reflect and enjoy life.

The flavours of difference,
imbibing culture that makes us who we are.
Beings of our surroundings,
at one with life,
but not stopping to absorb.

Too much work means I just see,
experience the bland.
I consume cardboard calories that are not fresh,
I,
not living for or in the moment.

I need to slow down from my fast food life.
Experience the crunchiness and veracity,
feel vitality,
absorb the vitamins of love,
friendship,
arguments and pain.

I must slow down and enjoy the spices of life and
relish the world.

Contrast

Part 1 – Lawyers

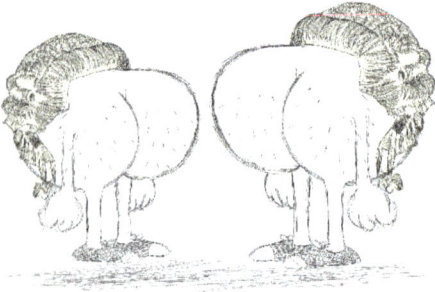

Conceited assholes,
never met a good'un;
talk by the minute charge by the hour,
always out to screw you.

Educated,
yes.
Conniving,
their very nature.
God complex,
a certainty.

They are clever,
too much for their own good as they twist and
turn truth to inflate the invoice.

Lawyers,
like terrible cough medicine,
necessary,
but you hate every minute of it.

Part 2- Firefighters

I look like you,
but feel like me;
we have the same decisions but come to different
conclusions.

When I see fire,
I worry,
run away,
call 999….
and you come.

You are an ordinary person,
just like me,
but who takes extraordinary risks…
for me.

You literally walk into the fiery valley of death,
into a burning house,
an inferno to save lives.

You put yourself in danger for the sake of others,
whereas I'm selfish,
inconsiderate,
don't worry about my loose joint,
the forgotten oil pan,
the burning joy-ride…

You are a hero,
a saviour,
a literal and figurative mask of oxygen,
the fireman's lift who gives chances to live another
day.

I salute you,
I honour you,
I'm inspired by you.

I wish I could have your courage,
fortitude,
strength of being,
strength of service,
strength of thinking about someone other than
yourself;
you are heroes.

Consultancy

Part 1

Entrepreneur or employee,
with a firm or freelance,
but always at the beck and call of your mistress-
the contract,
the client,
each changing,
never knowing what you'll do next,
with whom or where.

This is part of the joy,
the thrill of the unexpected,
of being a consultant.

Same deliverable different client;
different deliverable same client;
having to perform 100% all the time.

The challenges of consultancy:
blend into your clients' surroundings,
to exceed expectations,
to push yourself mentally and physically,
to take shit and let it roll of your shoulders,
your ideas… presented as theirs;
keeping your cool as others lose theirs.

Take out your emotion,
be impartial,
objective,
to be a jack of all trades and a subject matter
expert.
To blag expertise on everything,
to earn a contract,
to get repeat work,
to get paid while looking for your next mistress.

So, I walk once more into the den of lions,
not knowing who I'll work with or how it will go.

Its utter uncertainty,
risk and reward,

mental and emotional challenge,
project mange the assignment to complete on time
and within budget.

And then there is life…
marriage falling apart,
side-hustle not yet started,
parents' health,
other daily worries and fears,
all this while leading a team,
the first in two years.

Uncertainties are amplified.
Will I keep it together?
Can I listen, adapt, overcome?
Am I emotional resilient?

I have no choice but to go where David ventured,
accept my challenges head-on and not cower in the
face of adversity but use it as extra motivation,
to show myself what I'm capable of.

At 8:30am tomorrow,
the whistle will blow and over the top I will go.

The reality,
often I'm introduced…
and then the client will talk in the local language…
as they should;

I sit like a statue and ask myself,
what am I doing here?

I have my five minutes,
say my piece and make a presentation-
silence and boredom before,
silence and boredom after;
time to write this poem!

I catch words I understand but most I don't.
I read notes of what others have written.
I know what they talk about but not what they say.
I know what they should be saying,
but not if they are;
I ask myself,
what am I doing here?

I can't complain,
sitting like a mute,
daydreaming,
writing this poem!

I'm paid a lot of money as an 'expert',
but I'm not giving my 'expert' views,
so really, what am I doing here?

As the stoic philosopher Epictetus, said,
"the greater the difficulty,
the more glory in surmounting it.
Skilful pilots gain their reputation from storms and
tempests."
Not forgetting:
"circumstances don't make the man,
they only reveal him to himself."

Part 2

I've been lucky,
an interesting job that's taken me to the four cor-
ners of the world.

It's paid well and I get to experience much…
but that doesn't mean life's easy as sacrifices are
made and not always willingly.

I go to a country,
a culture,
like I've not experienced before.

Friendly people,
respectful and honest,
materialistic not hedonistic,
chilling, but little public socialising.
no womanising,
chatting,
back slapping,
plenty beer drinking but no panty dropping.

I have difficult bosses and clients.
I live in a suitcase and endless hotel rooms,
I'm constantly away from my children and have no
one to hold as I slip into sleep.
This is my life,
what it means to be an international consultant.

I don't,
can't let up.
There are few second chances when competition is
on the prowl;
business hard won should not be easily given up.

I always try to exce ed expectations,
push my limits,
life is sacrifice though I try to enjoy.

The older I get,
my satisfaction found in the next generation,
my bloodline,
they are why I persevere,
how I deflect insults and arrows,
how I can make their lot better.

Hotel Rooms for One

Hotel rooms are like fancy prison cells…
no friends or family to laugh with…
so I sit here or lie there,
brush my teeth or watch TV;
I'm eternally,
frustratingly bored.

What to do…
a film?
Work?
Order room service?
Read a book?
Masturbate with a chatroom girl?

Hotel rooms for one are far from an exciting,
a fun life,
so I will explore the night to chase away fears.

I briefly meet strangers in bars,
but this sliver of joy only reinforces,
nay, laughs at my loneliness.

Depression and anxiety set in so I…
drink like a fish,
eat chocolate by the ton,
fuck like a rabbit,
smoke like a chimney,
gamble as if I'm a millionaire,
get high as a kite…
my only control,
my release,
addiction to achieve accelerated sleep.

I go back to the hotel,
my temporary sanctuary,
a world where I'm only ever a visitor,
somewhere that I can never call home.

Why Do I Work This Way?

I am here
you there
life separating us,
work separating us,
but this is loving.

I think about you,
I want you,
but you are out of touch;
two hearts separated by oceans,
one life split by circumstance.

We are together in spirit if not body.
Our same hopes and dreams,
of remembering past times,
good times,
loving times.

We can't know what the future will bring,
if we will reunite or be apart,
reconsummate or share beds with others;
fate deciding our forever,
memories our past.

I'm sad and lonely,
its mid-afternoon,
my favourite day of the week,
Saturday.

I'm relaxing,
opened my first beer
making plans for the evening ahead.

Showered and dressed up,
pizza and three more beers consumed,
I'm feeling good,
my mojo up,
ready to hit the town in my lucky boxers.

A beer on the tram to keep my equilibrium,
that sweet spot of confidence,
where I can,

will talk to strangers,
for I have no friends in this new city,
my home for two weeks.

I refuse to be cowed by boredom and loneliness so
will make something happen.
I will build a life for myself,
my will greater than hindrances,
my depressing past,
my failing marriage;
my will,
will be done.

A couple of chats as hours pass,
drinks pass lips.
I can still walk straight,
I'm not slurring my words,
my hair still looks good and flirting has been fun,

Onto the main event-
a gathering of international strangers,
these my people.
Women I will try to wow with my daring do,
my light feet on the dance floor;
I Fred Astaire,
who will be my Ginger?

All too soon I stumble onto the tram,
alone,
the night fun but unsuccessful.
And so I drank,
and drank,
chatted,
and drank some more this to run from my de-
mons,
my self-loathing and insecurities,
but in so doing exposing my soul,
my real self,
the one who is worried about their looks,
fashion sense,
body image,
income level,

social status,
relationship status,
number of friends,
job security,
reliance on alcohol…

The booze doesn't lift me up,
it exposes,
brings my facade of confidence crashing down,
I so very transparent.

I cry for our smiles,
hopes.
expectation,
openness,
our past histories to be laughed and commiserated.

And then we fell apart,
away.

Love is tinged by reality,
uncertainty,
infidelity,
lack of unity,
no soul responsibility,
too much accountability,
pride before humility.

All that was sweet turned sour.
Our heat,
frozen.
Our relationship,
alive,
but not living-
reminiscing of yesteryears
rather than thinking of tomorrows.

We will survive,
we can persevere;
but what's been lost can't be rediscovered.

I cry for the what ifs,
the maybes and perhaps.

I contemplate what has been said,
done,
decided as this cannot be reversed or expunged.

Our choices are written in history,
destines designed,
fate waving her wand.

What will happen,
how life will unfold,
where you and I will be next I cannot tell-
ours,
a story of dreams,
star-crossed lovers,
ships that met in the night but got smashed in the
safety of port.

Maybe?
Maybe, there is hope;
maybe?

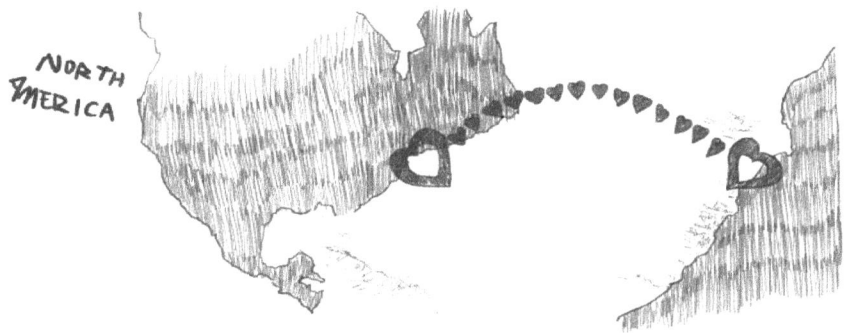

A Million Miles

It's been a month since I've seen my loved ones.
I'm home alone and sleeping by myself,
no wife to cuddle,
make me laugh,
light my life.

I'm a million miles from my family,
doing what I need to do as a man,
as a father,
my role predestined.

It's quiet,
too quiet.
No kids running around,
charging into the room,
shouting and jumping on the bed.
No school rush,
homework,
trips to the ice cream shop.

I enjoy my peace and quiet the first few days…
but then I'm alone,
not at home,
just somewhere I eat and sleep.

But what of me?
My boys not here,
my girl I can't comfort;
what sort of a man am I in a foreign field?

Away,
my mind on different realities to my normal.
Doing what I think is best,
but there is no right or wrong…
just life!

I love lives that I care for,
that I would die for,
lives that I'm doing this for,
lives,
my children,
that I'm not there for;
I'm twisting my melon.

My hymn:
get through the day,
do what I need to so I can do what I want to.

I found sisu in these times of questions,
uncertainty and loneliness.

I'm at the airport,
about to be reunited with my noisy crew.
their cheeky smiles,
their laughter,
all together again;
back to being a family.

Maid

So much happened in less than a minute...

One second, a maid,
working for a fancy Dan in a posh house,
I, a nobody,
a shadow to the elite,
an imposter in a rich house.

I was keeping quiet,
calm,
respectful,
doing what I need to feed my family,
to make it through the day.

And the next....

I'm an ignorant spic,
a worthless immigrant,
a moneyless thief,
a slave to the rich and powerful who use and abuse.

My boss wanted a portion of me,
one that I wasn't willing to give.

I am accused of stealing,
thieving,
pilfering.

I'll be found guilty as charged,
no judge nor jury,
no justice for him trying to take my body,
my virtue.

I will accept the punishment.
I will pray to god to get me through the terror of prison.
I will weep for my daughters.
I will keep my pride,
I will not hide the blood stained knife that protected my dignity.

Petty Theft

Whether you pick pockets,
take money from a fallen wallet or steal a Twix,
you're a thieving bastard.

I can't stand on my high-horse or I'll topple over.
I once stole a Mars Bar,
keep umpteen unpaid bills,
claimed a discount when there was none;
it felt good.

Save a penny,
make a pound…
but my gain was someone else's loss.

It wasn't my hard labour,
courage and perseverance to start and run a business.

Every Curly Whirly I stole diminished other's profits,
made it less likely they would employ someone,
give a first step into the adult world of work.

I wish I could give my Marathon back.

Hans

Is that lady walking an imaginary dog?
She has a lead,
a furrowed brow…
but no hound???

Is she loony-tunes,
a nutter,
her mind past its prime?
Alzheimer's?

Did she forget the pooch at home?

She delves into her shopping bag,
I don't know what will appear.
Strawberries?

A frozen chicken?
Tights?
A Chihuahua?
This is not,
rabbit from the hat time.

Out her hand comes,
slow and old…
like she is.

Her pinkies,
crinkled like an autumn leaf,
clutch a roll of tape;
that,
I never would have guessed!

She goes back in,
fumbles around,
her grey mitt,
veins bulging,
reappears holding papers;
the mind boggles.

With as much dexterity and grace as a
one flipper walrus,
she cellotapes her posters onto lampposts,
walls and trees.

I'm transfixed at the visage,
utterly befuddled as to what she's advertising.
A rave?
House-helper?
A lovely young man?

I have to investigate.

I saunter over confused and exhilarated,
a weird few minutes on my time space continuum.

Before I get to the sign,
I can see what's being searched...
more fool me...
her companion,
man's best friend,
her German Shepherd,
Hans.
The handsome beast,
photo tail wagging,
apparently gone missing.

I'm ashamed of my insolence,
lack of empathy.
I want to help the old lady,
the woman who could have been my mother,
my granny.

I take down the phone number and continue
walking;
karma sometimes has a way.

I walk and walk some more.

I sit on a bench,
ponder…
and then continue to wander.

I see a dog that looks suspiciously like
Hans,
but a German Shepherd…
in Germany,
hardly a surprise!

Another owner…
putting up notices on trees and lampposts...
has he also lost a dog?

I investigate a second time today.

It's tail wagging,
shopping bag sniffing Hans.
I finally get it;
he's been kidnapped,
200 Euro for his freedom!

In the Shadows

It's dark,
there's no need to hide,
I have nothing to fear,
but I keep to the shadows.

My eyes adjust to the dark,
I, on the lookout for my next opportunity.

I see an opening,
a window not fully wound up,
the vehicle just one in a long line.

I retreat further into the shadows,
I look up and down the street,
I bide my time.

Ten minutes,
the driver doesn't return,
no one comes back for a forgotten phone
or misplaced wallet.

I walk towards the car as if I'm the owner.
I take out my tools...
thirty seconds later, I'm in.
I crouch in the foot well,
hold my breath,
keep silent as my heart pounds my chest.

I'm buzzing,
adrenalin like acid flowing through my veins.

I check the glove box, nothing.
I slide my hand under the seats,
fingers touch the familiar shape of a phone.

My work done,
I check front then back;
no one around.

I stash the mobile in my jacket,
open the driver's door confidently,
the car mine.

I walk to a pub to sell my wares and buy a rewarding pint and celebrate a good night's work.

Eureka!

Fuuuuuuccckkkk!!!!

Where does a mother-fucker,
brother-trucker,
silly-ducker fucking start?

I have a thought,
a concept,
a bit of an idea,
a light bulb moment...
but how do I turn my project into a money-spin-
ner,
winner winner chicken dinner,
without it becoming a head-spinner?

I make a list,
write a pitch so others get the gist,
see my inspiration,
collation,
jubilation...
truth be told,
it came from inebriation.

I fret,
I fold,
my tea shop genius soon gold…
but what I thought would be easy,
now seems old.

I love,
I hate,
can't decide which side of the plate the but-
tered-side of the toast will land,
my dedication...
could quite possibly lead to ruination.

God damn,
I thought I had something there,
here,
everywhere fucking where.

My brain going Caesar,
salad not Julius.
I have no strategy as I think how to implement,
look for complement,
somehow cement into reality,
clarity,
I need humility.

Business is sink or swim,
jump the deep end,
hike Everest as nothing is impossible.

I need confidence not arrogance,
partnership not go alone,
believe,
have hope not fear,
won't hold back,
but take control and start my business.

Business Case

Do you know your business fundamentals-
What are the business drivers?
What problem are you solving?
Who is the customer?
What can you do better or unique?
Who are the competition?
Is there a sustainable business case?
Do you know the financial drivers of the business-.
your cost and revenue models?

This is not sexy stuff,
but is fundamental,
elemental,
not coincidental to success or failure,
missteps or growth.

The numbers don't lie!
They are not a spy but a reflection of reality;
you might think banality,
but that will be your calamity if not taken seriously.

So, trust in the process,
the numbers.
Set key performance indicators and
make an implementation plan to follow.

Business is not easy,
not everyone an entrepreneur...
understand the fundamentals to give yourself a fighting chance!

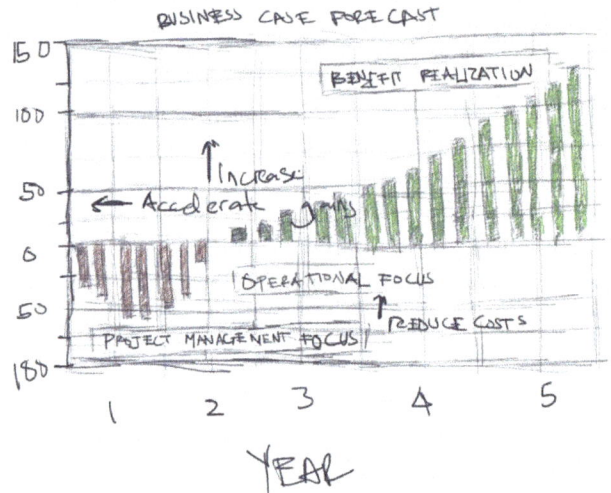

Entrepreneur

A thought,
an idea is nothing without a plan,
finance and sales;
this,
a truth all entrepreneurs know.

A gold-plated toaster,
a wonder drug,
DJing,
growing veggies,
building holiday homes or establishing a tea shop…
all are viable businesses,
all are subject to customers' whim,
the entrepreneur's ability to convince.

Ideas are cheap,
boasts are transparent,
and if you can't sell you have no business.

Finalise your strategy,
decide how to implement,
organise your suppliers,
design your marketing,
start production and hire employees.

The entrepreneur is the embodiment of the business,
the heart, brain and soul of the enterprise,
the person accountable to stakeholders,
the key determinant of success.

A heavy weight rests on their shoulders.
They are responsible for success,
salaries,
job satisfaction and security,
customer happiness.

This is what it takes to start and run a business,
it's as simple as that,
as hard and harsh as that!
I won't lie to you,
my friend,
my soon to be entrepreneur.

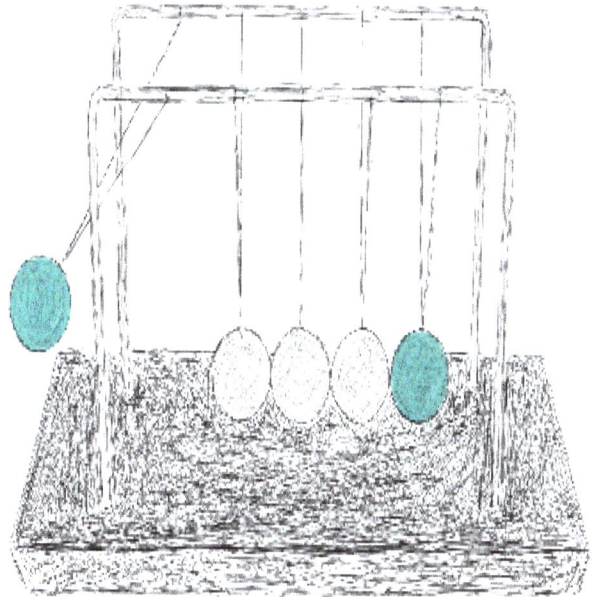

Money Makes the World go Round

I sell food cans,
veggies,
anything that makes me a buck,
I, the Essex Bezos.

I'm uneducated but not useless.
I need a hand up not a handout.
I know business,
supply and demand,
where my margins are made.

I'm hustling and bustling,
looking for any new angle,
new opportunity.

Cash is my king,
queen and jack,
my sadomasochistic mistress,
I her slave,
doing whatever I need for my family.

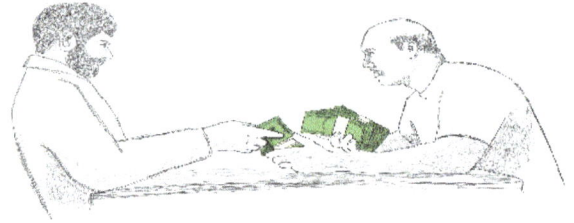

Leadership

What is a leader
and who do they lead?

Is it position,
salary or life experience?

What makes someone a leader and others follow-
ers,
sheep corralled by shepherd?

Are leaders born or made?
Nature or nurture,
parentage or in-built desire,
robustness,
cussedness,
don't give a fuckedness as long as the goal is
achieved,
the objective mastered and overcome?

Why take responsibility for others,
make them believers in you,
you who gives then belief that no mountain is too
high to conquer,
sea too rough to swim.

A leader is the one who can pull along the team,
each member an integral part to the whole,
if one falls you all fail.

They are the captain of the ship and chart the
course for success.
They have the elixir,
the magic potion,
the je ne sais quoi that is charisma,
the vital ingredients to lead,
to be a leader.

Charisma

Mr Charisma,
Ms X Factor,
the persona that can't be taught or bought.

The winner from the bottom of the pile,
the person others want to be,
the one in a hundred,
or should that be million,
who never, says, "never."

The leader who always goes forward,
never backwards.
Others will follow and fight for them in the
boardroom,
on the rugby pitch,
on the field of battle.

The risk taker giving it everything,
leaving nothing in reserve.
"All or nothing," their mantra.
Living life on the edge.
"Today not tomorrow,"
their way of living;
their favourite question,
"if not now, when?"

Mr Charisma,
Ms X Factor.
the person who when thrown to the wolves comes
back leader of the pack.

Mentor

I look at you and hope to see me,
not now,
now not my time,
buy if I work hard,
take calculated risks,
make wise investments and keep my shit together...
maybe one day.

You are a visionary,
friendly,
kind-hearted and willing to help me,
support me achieve what you already have.

You have faults,
weaknesses;
nobody perfect.
A failed marriage,
kids who don't return calls,
business failures as much as successes,

but this is what makes you strive to be the best,
to understand experience,
the good and bad in life,
to accept challenges and take advantages of opportunities;
this is living,
loving life.

We have known each other for some time,
but I don't,
can't know all of you.

I consider you a friend,
would like you to be my mentor,
to give advice when I ask,
to be a pillar when I'm struggling,
to celebrate my successes as I yours,
to guide how I should council others.

LGBTQ+

One of the most significant transformations to the UK in my lifetime is the evolution of sexual freedoms. Where before it was repression, the media portraying sexuality in a narrow, sensationalized manner and, bat-eared razzle mags, now everyone can freely express themselves. As a heterosexual male, my outlook on sexual diversity has radically changed from uncomprehending diversity to being an advocate for sexual liberty.

There's nothing like being in a minority / experiencing discrimination (in my case a mixed-race marriage) to understand the trials and tribulations of being different. Who you love should never be a social disadvantage or make you a target for ridicule, or worse, ostracism and stigma. The rainbow as the symbol of LGBTQ+ pride and celebrating sexual acceptance and inclusivity is perfect iconology; it encapsulates the vibrant spectrum of identities. This next set of poems celebrates sexual acceptance.

A Hundred Shades of Rainbow Love

Love in its many forms,
all shapes, sizes and Technicolor glory.
Each to their own,
determining what the heart desires.

Girls loving boys,
boys loving boys,
boys loving girls,
girls loving girls and the 1,000 colours in between,
a rainbow of sexuality.

Same gender,
same race,
same age,
same kinks,
none of the above,
all the above and the 1,000 colours in between,
a rainbow of sexuality.

Two in a relationship ,
three,
more?
1,000 colours of love where there is no right or wrong,
where what is complicated to others represents
honesty are truth to the only ones who matter,
In a hundred shades of rainbow love.

Turquoise

Turquoise
Walking,
walking,
drinking,
contemplating not stalking a woman who's sun-kissed,
bad-ass dressed,
turquoise hair blessed.

She stops,
perches her posterior pleasantly,
pleasingly on the periphery of a post box.

I'm not staring,
feeling excruciating,
wild gesticulating or body shaming....
for I'm now combobulating,
realising that she's a he,
grey beard flaunting,
we,
both anticipating the night ahead.

We start talking,
giggling,
gossiping,
conversationing,
laughing,
delighting in the other,
living,
both in the mood for jubilating,
celebrating.

I'm soon to be parting from the woman of grey beard and turquoise hair,
each into the sun-kissed night we go.

Pam

I'm nature and nurture,
culture and couture,
a mix,

I decide my ethics,
love and hates,
my reason for being.

No one tells me how to live,
not my teacher
my church
my family
my friends…
though I will listen,
respect,
agree to disagree.

I meet my Tinder,
I'm 41 not 31,
married 10 years,
divorced in 10 weeks.

On my profile…
business dealer,
far realer,
window cleaner.

I'm flirting with a woman,
Pam,
she has plan to be a man,
Stan,
turn from she to he,
she who is attracted to me…
we both living lies.

Is my sexuality,
a strategy,
a tragedy or just reality?

The contours of my body
lumps,

bumps and protrusions,
I know so well.

You can have no idea,
or do you…
an inkling,
that I'm a transvestite?

You stare,
your eyes drawn to my enhanced cleavage,
my smile,
my long legs and of wonders to come,
of the night untold.

I look at you,
I see excitement of the unknown,
of bodies to be discovered
of minds read and present shared.

Charlie

Born a boy,
male on his passport.
sticks as guns and rugby his sport;
Charlie was a boys' boy.

He hit teenage years,
desires to be with a girl strong,
to feel what it's like to lie with a female,
smell her perfume,
stroke smooth skin,
feel the fabric of delicate clothes.

Fighting society's norms,
religious doctrine and mocking peers,
Charlie can't deny his loving,
longing and lusting to dress as a woman,
and feel a man.
To hold masculinity in her arms,
to feel vulnerable and protected,
experience true love from her heart,
give all she can to another.

Charlie keeps her unisex name.
Half-man, half-woman,
the forever battle of a female persona within a male body,
but now at peace,
no longer pretending.

Non-Binary

Born a man or woman,
male or female,
boy or girl...
these,
a life in a black and white world,
but, I'm a human being,
non-binary and trying to make my way through life.

Told who I should be by parents,
by friends,
religion,
laws,
by the world,
expectations,
everybody's but mine!
but, I'm a human being,
non-binary and trying to make my way through life.

My reality is my own,
I need to be free not live through others.
I will be who I am,
not living a lie.
I'm a human being,
non-binary and trying to make my way through life.

You have challenges as do I.
You have insecurities...
but don't put them on me.
We are human beings,
trying to make our way through life.

Who I love or hate,
rejoice in or battle with...
if I'm your friend,
stand by my side,
don't sit in judgement,
castigate,
love me as I'm a human being,
trying to make my way through life.

Your decision-
do you want to be in my life?

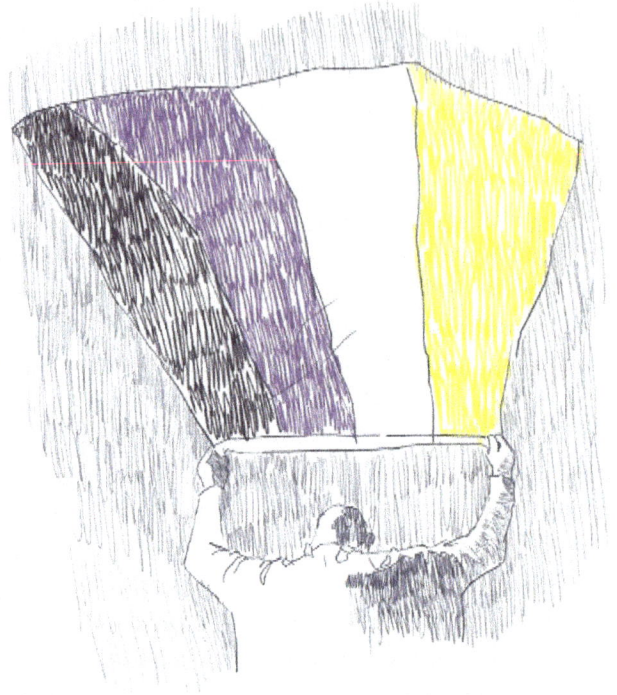

Hiding

I look at you and don't know what I see.
I was brought up in an analogue world of black
and white T.V.,
There was right and wrong,
positive and negative,
male and female,
gay and straight.

It was a time when options were limited,
being who you truly are not on the menu…
apart from the courageous,
the honest truth-tellers.

Those who could be themselves,
could envisage a different life,
one of completeness,
of doing the right thing for themselves,
of expressing their truth,
of being gender fluid,
taking the best of both worlds
as their soul dictates.

I can't pretend to understand,
but I do accept,
admire,
jealous of someone who fully understands
who they are,
more than I know my own reality,
more than I can be proud to live my
strengths and forgive my weaknesses.

I must also be true to myself,
not give a fake smile to the world,
to people who don't care about me,
but who I try to please so conform.

Manila

A new airport,
a new day,
a new city
a new entry on my time space continuum.

Manila,
city of the Pinay,
traffic and smog.

Come for a conference,
learn more about myself.

Have some beers,
a business meeting or two.
a backstreet massage,
a lady boy's passage.

Keep an open mind to the next experience,
the next place,
the next person in your life.

Alarm Cock

I'm here,
now,
a heterosexual man,
jigging my jive,
alive,
living my life,
night spinning,
alcohol drinking.

In this moment,
this time,
not wanting to wait,
forget,
to put today into tomorrow,
next year,
not worrying of the what to come.

Meet a man,
a woman,
a someone I'm attracted to,
a night of adventure,
hedonism,
bodies to unite.

We kiss,
bite,
lick and excite.
We sweat and fall asunder,
thunder until lightening gone.

Wake,
the alarm cock ringing,
desire stinging,
wanting,
needing,
some more fucking,
hate the reality,
new day banality,
life feeling finality
waiting until the next alarm cock.

Love

I am a man like you in almost every way.
We look the same,
bleed the same,
have good times the same,
but I am a convict and you are not.
You can love who you want,
I cannot;
why?

Why am I treated differently?
Why do human rights not apply to me?
Why can't I love my fellow man?
Who gives you the right to abuse,
ostracise,
insult and imprison?

Why are you responsible for my happiness?
Who are you to decide what I can or can't do in the privacy of my house?
Why can't I show the world my lover,
my best friend,
my soulmate?

I have not been invaded by the devil.
I too believe in holy books.
I love my neighbour.
I'm no murderer,
paedophile or rapist,
not even a looter,
and yet you treat me harshly for being me.

Where is your humanity
humility,
paternity,
maternity,
sense of respectability,
understandability?

I am responsible for my actions.
I stand proud for who I am.
I wish all to prosper in a free society,
where everyone can be who they are;
let me live free,
that's all I ask!

The Worst

Is there such a thing,
as, the worst?
Does one stand above the others,
something so despicable,
so inhumane that you can't face yourself?

Have you ever felt or caused such hurt,
such anger generated meaning innocents are
caught in the maelstrom?

What's the worst thing you've done?
Can it beat my dreadful deed,
the curse I put on another due to my inadequacies?

It's a sin I live with every day,
a regret I'll take to my grave.
Every time I look in the mirror I see Imran's
ghostly visage,
hear his infectious laugh.

I want to reach out and touch him.
To say, sorry,
to beg for clemency.
This guilt is one I rightly deserve.
I was not able to accept my weaknesses,
failings and insecurities.

I am reaping what I sowed,
my nightmares invaded by Imran's apparition,
his glorious smile.

Truth be told,
I could never accept his forgiveness as I never
accepted his friendship
of him being his true self,
of loving another man.

Why did I refuse to accept this is who he was?
Why did I spit his friendship back in his face?

May my soul stay cursed,
so I never forget to be accepting.

Another Hundred Shades of Rainbow Love

Not my place,
not my time,
here by circumstance
to pass minutes away.

I'm married,
have children…
and I'm in a gay club,
amongst fags,
bum boys…

It's my choice,
my decision to be here,
now,
in the unknown,
but not on my own.

I'm amongst honest men,
free men,
freer than me.

They're living their truth,
living life,
proud of who they are,
who they represent,
not hiding or ashamed.

I look and see smiles,
dancing bodies;
they're freedom personified,
not a contorted mind like mine.

I'm confused,
lonely.
I have no body to jive with,
smile to light up…
and I don't want to be alone,
to sleep alone,
tonight.

Am I on the lookout?

For what?
girls,
women…
men…
maybe?

I've never been with a man;
would everything feel wrong,
would it feel right?

Bob Dylan through speakers,
times, there are a changing,
this the perfect song for this time,
this place of my journey of enlightenment.

All I want is to give love and feel loved,
for my heart to be free with the one I love.

Each man and women,
boy or girl,
should have the right to live their life and love who
they desire,
have a soulmate,

Whether gay or straight,
white or black,
young or old,
man or woman,
there is no right or wrong when you're in love,
when you live your truth,
when you're free.

Acceptance

The sun barely visible,
I put the next beer to my lips,
a new day,
the night not over,
life continues.

I don't know the future…
other than bars to explore,
people to chat,
experiences to be had.

Walk the lonely road,
hear music behind closed door,
an unknown world…
I enter.

I'm met by a bar counter of males,
the rainbow flag passing me by.
I'm out of place,
a stranger in a strange land...
in a strange bar...
all foreign...
but don't care so long as conversation,
of new experiences,
of hearing of a different life,
gay or straight,
LGBTQ+ sexual alphabet soup,
as long as it's great.

I'm not good at sitting in a corner by myself,
I don't always want company,
but company needs to want me!

Need to make myself known,
find someone to chat with.
as I'm a man and fancy a bird,
a lass,
a chick,
some fanny,
punani.
I don't the know the homosexual equivalent…
a bit of alright?

some good looker?
handsome man?

But,
what's more important,
now,
today,
is that I'm accepted,
welcomed into a den that's not normally mine.

I take a seat,
busy table,
start a random chat with 2 gays,
3 lesbians and 1 bohemian lady.

They welcome me,
a random stranger into their circle,
this,
a magical mystery tour,
my mind saying,
this is my place.

I must follow my philosophy of understanding,
not being prejudiced.
being taught acceptance.
I,
who hold that sacred,
am a preacher from that gospel;
for where there's life,
life shall prevail.

Sounds like a bible quote...
but just my harmony as I learn to accept what I
don't understand.
what I've never experienced,
accept that acceptance is good karma,
that new friends have truths to unveil

I will have no regrets as I enter a new world,
no look backs,
this is my now,

my choices,
my life lessons that have brought me here,
this point on my time space continuum,
this place where I don't know my future,
where my present is opaque,
my past black,
my future one of unknown possibilities,
but by accepting,
anything is possible.

Is There Another Way?

Life is for living,
exploring and experiencing new sights and sounds,
tastes and feels;
I want,
need,
sensory overload.

Known each other five years,
married three.
A monogamous life for two,
monotony,
the challenge I fear the most,
fun so fleeting,
self-hate and depression overtaking.

Once, we had such smiles,
such hope.
expectation,
openness,
past histories were to be laughed at and
commiserated over.

Love was...
tinged by reality,
uncertainty,
but there was also unity,
joint responsibility,
accountability,
humility,
not pridability.

Life is for living,
exploring and experiencing new sights and sounds,
tastes and feels;
I want,
need,
sensory overload.

Now I'm on the edge,
heart-broken,
soul drained;
when will the lawyer call?

All that was sweet,
turned sour.
Our heat,
frozen.

Our relationship,
alive,
but not living,
We reminisce of yesteryears rather than thinking
of tomorrows.

I don't know the future,
but is divorce better than this misery,
insult and conspiracy,
fists and shouting;
this no way to live.

Your mind made up,
please, no emotional blackmail.
Open your mind,
maybe your heart will follow?

Life is for living,
exploring and experiencing new sights and sounds,
tastes and feels;
I want,
need,
sensory overload.
We had so much fun together,
a future of possibility
nothing was impossibility,
not when I'd found my soulmate,
my best friend forever,
you.

We had each other,
we had our dreams,
we had our children . . .
but still you wanted more,
100 percent of me,
this more than I could give.

It's not the lies that cut me to the bone,
nor the constant competition,
you always having to be right,
always better than me.
It's not even the falling respect,
emotional neglect,
it's that you always pretended to be something
you're not.

Your sense of entitlement,
suffocating,
your constant excuses
utterly draining.
The chip on your shoulder,
too big to remove.
You can never admit mistakes,
never…
but always the first to point fingers.

Our time is over,
for none of the above…
It's the deception,
taking me as a fool.
money that's gone missing,
funds I sweated for our family,
to give life,
opportunity,
future possibility for our children,
that's what killed us.

You thieved,
were too pig-headed,
selfish,
decided to take,
steal.

But, understand this,
what you really took was our happiness,
time together,
time with the children.
What you really took
was not pounds, dollars or euros,
but our family's future;
that's unforgivable!

Life is for living,
exploring and experiencing new sights and sounds,
tastes and feels;
I want,
need,
sensory overload.

My dear,
you will always be close in my heart

no matter the barbs,
We have history,
children together,
but what you now offer I no longer want.

I want laughter not lectures,
a common direction and respect,
not each doing their own.
To appreciate the others efforts,
not be taken for granted.

Can you accept this,
realise and rationalise this?
That no matter wedding bells and happy ever
afters,
one person can't meet all the needs of another.

It's not about dents in pride,
nor owning someone,
a marriage certificate is but a piece of paper,
a willingness of two souls to share their time on
this earth…
If that past it's sell-by-date,
change must be a coming.

Life is for living,
exploring and experiencing new sights and sounds,
tastes and feels;
I want,
need,
sensory overload.

Will we survive,
maybe?
We can preserve,
persevere,
but this is not living;
what has been lost can't be rediscovered,
but can be reimagined
rediscovered,
reengineered if both sides willing.

I cry for the what ifs,
the maybes and perhaps,
knowing,
what has been said,
done,
decided,
can't be reversed
expunged.

Choices have been written in history,
destines designed,
fate weaving her wand;
I will not drown in your bitterness,
swallowed as you gobble our marriage.

Ours is a story of dreams,
romance,
star crossed lovers,
ships that met in the night
but got smashed in the safety of a port.
If there is a way forward,
maybe,
now is the time to accept three in our relation-
ship…
or accept divorce.

Maybe?
Maybe,
timbers can be found to start re-building,
that can used as foundations.

What will happen next,
how life will unfold,
where you and I will be,
I can't tell,
all I know,
life is for living,
exploring and experiencing new sights and sounds,
tastes and feels;
I want,
need,
sensory overload.

TECHNOLOGICAL RELATIONSHIPS

During my childhood, technology used to mean a crappily made Doctor Who Darlicks; it's a far cry from the shiny gadgets of nowadays. At the heart of this revolution is the smartphone, the king that rules our life. Studies claim, that we look at the little screen 200 times a day; it's omnipresent and records our every movement. Our data is analysed and magically appears pixilated as adverts for services that we didn't know we needed or people with similar interests. As the saying goes, if the service is free, you are the product! I can't imagine life without the little bugger. It would be very difficult to opt out of this mind-bending existence where everything is recorded, nothing forgotten. I believe the tiny marvel is the Trojan Horse that will either usher in the end of the state or fulfil the vision of the Silicon Valley unicorns and other techno-miracle workers, shape-shifters, wizards and prophets. The dopamine driven phenomena of social media, and which is intricately intertwined with our daily lives, I believe is incompatible with mental wellbeing. Technology and globalisation are catalysers for heightened anxiety and depression. It's no wonder an increasing number of people feel lonely. Even if one has a million friends in the digisphere it means nothing if there isn't one person who you can call up anytime, night or day, and go out for a jar with to celebrate, commiserate or just talk shit with for a few hours.

Maybe, you'll label me a technophobe, but the dystopian futures envisioned in Mad Max, the Matrix, Blade Runner and The Hunger Games now seem not so far away. The recent accelerated advances in 3D printing, Cryptocurrency, Blockchain, artificial intelligence and, virtual and augmented reality, means we are now only years away from that future. Will our monkey brains - that adapt at evolutionary speed - be able to cope? This question, my friends, in the true quandary of our age.

My Electronic Life

A digital me,
a digital you,
a digital here,
a didgeridoo.

From our aboriginal ancestors yesterday,
to our virtual reality today…
and who knows what tomorrow?

I'm flesh and bones with a digital identity –
does this make me code or a lost soul in cyber-
space?

Do others see me the way I present myself
through Facebook updates,
Tweets and Instagram photos?

Do I pretend to be something I'm not?
Why do I always put my best…
or fake foot forward?
Is it to make others envious,
jealous?
Am I so insecure that I lie to be validated?

We are social animals needing to belong,
yet live further apart,
isolated and rely on technology to keep socially
connected;
isn't this the definition of irony?

As for my Facebook friends,
what do we really know of each other?
I know you have a cat,
are 37,
a woman…
but are you actually a 73-year-old, dog-loving man?

Is quality or quantity more important?
What does 100 Facebook "likes" from 1,000
"friends" really mean?
I prefer chatting with a mate,
over a beer,

seeing their face,
reading their body language,
hearing the tone of their voice
and using my sixth sense to understand their feel-
ings and emotions…
and what is not said.

In the modern world…
social (media) pain is as real as physical pain;

Modern life is making us lonelier…
even though we're more connected!

Is a digital life, real,
or, just something like it?

Faithful Friend

My phone,
my trusty companion that will
find me random bars,
a chipper,
karaoke or stripper.

My faithful friend is my
confessional and diary,
communicator,
bank and juke box.

It has a life-changing capacity…
my women more interested in the
screen than me,
flattered more by Facebook
flatulence than everyday reality.

The mobile,
my electronic life,
mind-reader,
mind-bender,
future life generator,
the analogue world…
rear-view mirror,

My battery's dead-
bugger.

Am I Turning Binary?

Life is changing in front of my eyes,
literally on a smartphone, laptop or tablet.
Browse my folders and files,
you will see into my soul;
my gadgets,
electronic witnesses to my life.

Do I understand who I am or where in the world I
belong?
To be alive, today,
has different meaning to 20, 50, 500 years ago.

I'm no longer fighting battles with swords,
I'm a binary human,
my work,
my loves and probably my death,
recorded in a world of 0s and 1s

You can know the music I love,
an eclectic mix of dance and trance,
sixties and seventies, guitars;
no Bieber, no boy bands.
Know my opinion and theories.
Read my novels, my poems, my emails.
Look at photos and see friends and family,
where I have travelled,
the birth of my children.

My financial goings on:
my once hoped investment plans,
current cash flow problems,
depressing bank statements.

Whether you see into my world
by hacking my email,
pick-pocketing my smartphone or stealing my
laptop,
you will know more about me than my closest
friends-
maybe even me!

But my life is not just megabytes.
My digital self doesn't tell you how I feel in the
moment when dancing on tables,
making love,
playing with my daughter,
working, chatting or laughing.

You can know my digital life,
but it's better you know me and I know you...
in the analogue world!

Connected?

I have 1,000 Facebook connections,
but how connected am I?
Is a connection through a copper wire a real-world
interaction?

Someone has been: born, graduated, died.
Five seconds to type, well done or sorry,
wish I was with you-
does that mean anything,
or it's the quickest, cheapest,
most insincere form of acknowledgement?

Do you take a like to mean something more than
ten seconds,
two seconds of attention,
nothing more than a fleeting thought?

The value,
quite literally of time,
is getting twisted.
If I make time to meet you,
or someone makes time to meet me,
that is now considered generous,
not, being a friend.

They say,
you are born to family but make friends;
in this day and age,
is that digital irony?
Does 100 likes make you a liked person?

Do you post out of pride or to make others jeal-
ous?
Is what you posted a true representation of your
life or a photoshopped version?
Do your digital friends know the difference
or care about the metamorphosis?

For a job well done,
does a like make you proud?
Is a Facebook like one percent of the meaning
of a congratulatory slap on the back?

I like you or I don't.
You like me or you don't.
In a digital world,
it's difficult to tell one from the other.
In reality,
not of the virtual or augmented kind,
we shake hands and part company;
it's our human interconnection
that decides if we meet again.

We are ever more digitally connected,
there is no doubt about that;
but connected to what or who?
1,000 friends who I've never met,
who have never seen me at my best or worse.
Who've never seen excel or be an idiot.
A digital friend,
in a digital world,
but who can't give me human
time, irony, scorn or love.

I can have digital friends,
digital romance,
even digital sex...
but not someone to hold in my arms,
to feel their heart beat,
to taste their smell
to feel intimacy.

Modern life,
an irony of being ever more connected
but with fewer connections.

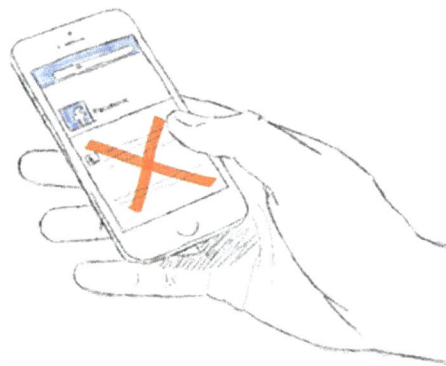

Selfie

Instagrammer looking fab,
doing cool,
showing muscles,
Buddha's and fun times.

Living a photoshopped life,
a life that's not mine, not theirs.
Showing only the good,
never the bad,
certainly no ugly.

A fan-tiddly-tastic utopia of lies;
a life that's not real to you,
to me.

A lie that engineers jealousy,
envy,
self-envy;
jealous of the fake life portrayed.

I have followers,
but I would rather be happy and honest,
a real me.

Unicorn Influencers

My world no longer limited to a dial in a red box,
now we have a library,
a camera,
a world in our pockets;
communications,
relations,
life and love digitized.

I'm 19 and finding my way in the world-
education or business?
I ask myself,
or is business my education?

Can I be an entrepreneurial teacher to my Luddite,
technophobe father?
He,

who has no idea of modern life;
his,
an unconditional hate of social media.

My world
is the world of friends and followers,
likes and shares,
where I'm confident to learn, see and hear,
to express myself and be authentic.

But, that doesn't mean I can't earn.
I need independence,
to be proud of what I've achieved,
to have a sense of self-worth in an unpredictable
world.

I use Snapchat,
Facebook;
I'm a Bomber,
a digital native,
sharing, my medium.

Don't hate me for being an influencer,
don't be jealous of my commercial contracts
or places I visit,
clothes I'm given or parties attend…
this is my work,
my job as much as being a butcher,
baker or candlestick maker.

We are the youth of the 21st century and there are
new rules to play by!

I don't need your envy.
I try not to be jealous of those more successful.
I have insecurities like you,
worries like you,
shit happens in my world also…
I'm left to the caprice of the number of
likes I generate.

I'm just trying to make it through life.

Viral Pumpkin Head

The sun no longer has his hat on,
leaves are falling,
the weather's gone shitty;
we are truly in Autumn.

The wind blowing,
rain slanting,
days shortening;
soon fireworks exploding.

Taken from American cousins,
dress ups and pumpkins,
trick or treating,
All Souls too boring.

I play the fool,
stick a pumpkin on my head.

Banter goes awry,
social media goes viral,
fun memories forever.

I'm Steve Austin

Will I be a Steve Martin brain,
a six-million dollar man,
a Matrix of ones and zeros,
or human skin and bones as we approach a Black Mirror future?

I'm a homosapien,
a DNA cousin to monkeys,
only generations away from swinging in trees
and roaming the savannah.

To run was how we were designed,
evolved,
sweating sweetly to race down prey.
That's what made us unique,
the ultimate bad ass…
who's now subservient to AI corporations.

I'm a version of my parents,
but no longer someone they would recognise;
I'm a hybrid-
science fiction and humanity collided.

My arms are metal,
legs carbon fibre;
bionic eyes decide which worlds I enter.

My limbs built by corporations.
My innards insured.
My mind owned by a finance house.
My fate algorithmically foretold.

The one world government made us bionic,
enforced us to give up our soul,
to deny our humanity and reverse the essence of being alive.

I am no longer what,
who or how I was born–
I'm Steve Austin,
the 6-million-dollar man.

Faustian State

I'm home,
the country of my birth,
but this island where inequality
and The Score rules,
where liberty is not evenly dispensed,
doesn't feel like mine anymore!

Here,
now,
is a corner of a foreign field.
Though it's familiar in many ways,
I'm now a stranger,
a foreigner,
a fish out of water.

Where I knew chaos,
it is now regimented.
Where I experienced uncertainty,
there is order.
There is no spontaneity and even less freedom.

We are told what to buy,
how to behave and where to go…
it is not the life I've been accustomed to,

one of disappointment and frustration,
this a price I'm willing to pay to feel like I'm living,
of being overjoyed by small wins.

I'm used to bars being small and intimate,
a hive of what might be,
not caring about the morrow,
filled with all social and financial classes…

In the UK,
there's no mixing between the elite and the masses.
In Africa,
there is stark disparity,
but all know the family village,
their roots,
to give respect to elders irrespective of wealth.

British families are nuclear but separated,
little common ground,
no time for empathy or helping others.

I'm a Brit who's lived in Africa…
but now feel I'm a Malawian living in the UK.

Life or Something Like It

Humans are social animals needing to belong,
yet now we live a digital life
where nuclear families are atomised,
relationships more superficial,
vaporised.

We live apart and rely on social technology,
modern life = digital irony,
we are more connected yet lonelier,
more isolated.

My digital pain is as real as physical pain.
I have social media but not a social network.
I expose only what I want,
make belief perfection,
never the bad or ugly.

We seek digital friendships to reduce our analogue pain.
We get a Facebook like from a new friend,
but not the like of seeing someone's face,
interpreting inner feelings,
body language and tone of voice.

We are homosapien with animal instincts.
From climbing trees and roaming savannahs,
we lived in a social pack;
social interaction is in our DNA.
Now more than ever,
the idea of what it means to be human is moving,
the world around us, changing.

Is a digital life a real life,
or just something like it?

A FINAL THOUGHT

Money makes the world go around. One simple question you can ponder: who is leveraging whom? Are others leveraging your time or, are you leveraging theirs? If you are going to be an entrepreneur, here's a few lessons I've picked up over the years.

1. Find the right people to work with.
2. Move fast. Get on with it rather than let the business die of procrastination.
3. It's better to do something wrong, quick and cheap and learn lessons, rather than trying to achieve perfection.
4. Follow an iterative development process. Always seek feedback from the customer, staff and your networks. Don't think you know it all – spoiler alert – you don't.
5. Be persistent. Have the perseverance of a bull elephant. Accept each challenge that comes at you from every which angle.
6. It is vital to find purpose in life; without it, life is empty. Therefore, understand your stakeholder's (customers, staff, spouse, supplier etc.) purpose and motivation to interact with you; this will help in building a viable value proposition.
7. Small problems are small. Don't make them into something they're not as that can catalyse self-fulfilling destruction.
8. Have an inner compass. Know how you see yourself and your contribution to the world; this is central to the human condition.
9. Discover what you enjoy, you'll put your heart and soul into it. If you love what you do, it's not work or a chore!

However you earn your bread, finance, is ultimately the root of the immigration / multiculturalism question. Therefore, the critical analysis, is, do those who do not originate from the UK (including second and third generation migrants) contribute or take away from the overall financial, social and cultural well-being of the country? Where many view diversity as a plus, a significant number perceive it negatively. Perhaps, in the near future, with the existential challenges of technological advancement and climate change, it will compel us to band together and unite to find common solutions. Alternatively, the challenges might foster greater populism and inwards looking attitudes, this resulting in the creation and then persecution of scapegoats.

Despite the uncertainties, I maintain hope for the future. The world knows what needs to done. The challenge, are there enough visionary leaders with the political will to reduce emissions, level economic inequality, reverse environmental degradation and unleash innovation. Leaders who prioritise humanity over their own political survival? The two are not incompatible, indeed the opposite. If we don't find solutions, society at large will look for scapegoats, including the leaders. Blame will be apportioned on those who are different from the majority whether based on ethnicity, religion, sexual preference, wealth, politics or many of the other freedoms which modern

Brits now take for granted. Let us not walk into the dystopian future where our thoughts and beliefs are dictated to us.

Thank you, dear reader, my friend for being on this poetic journey. I hope through my experiences I have given you a new perspective on life. So, I say, never blame your circumstances. A positive mind-set will always lead to a more fortuitous outcome than a negative approach. One should not fear failure; it happens- get up and give it another lash. Don't be ashamed of your mistakes; learn from them. We all screw-up, accept this is part of life. Embrace experience, good or bad; there is always something to be learned. If you don't go after what you want, you will never have it. If you don't ask, the answer is always no. If you don't step forward, you will remain in the same place. Be curious and have a willingness to engage with the unknown. Questioning does not show weakness but is rather a sign of strength, a true measure of intelligence. Open yourself to the world and express that you aren't afraid to exhibit your ignorance but want to learn, search for knowledge and truth from those who can educate and guide. "By doubting we are led to question, by questioning we arrive at the truth." Peter Abelard, 1079- 1142

Soar Like an Eagle

I'm a bi-woman,
coloured lady,
from foreign lands before;
my business isn't shady,
I'm ready to entrepreneur.

I work from home,
I'm not alone,
my man emotionally sustains me.

I search for help,
a business team to comprehend,
my faith to enlighten,
an open society to support.

I get loans,
my enterprise booms,
I save and excel,
soar like an eagle.

I now employ,
my children enjoy,
I am flying.

My dear husband,
your love transcends,
together,
we're never failing.

Thank you,
the UK for giving,
let me help others believing.

A NEW YOU
SPA & SALON

ABOUT THE AUTHOR

I'm an entrepreneur & business consultant by day, novelist & poet by night. The son of a British Army officer, I volunteered in rural Tanzania in 1997 before going to university to study marketing. I have lived and worked in Ethiopia, Germany, Kenya, Jordan, Ireland, Malawi, Saudi Arabia, Tanzania and the UK over the last 25 years, my varied experiences of culture, relationships, food, music and everything else that makes the world go round, the source of my inspiration.

www.ingramcontent.com/pod-product-compliance
Lightning Source LLC
Chambersburg PA
CBHW081552040426
42448CB00016B/3296